T0316471

ALMOND IN PETERHOUSE

ALMOND
IN PETERHOUSE

and other poems

BY

FRANKLIN KIDD

CAMBRIDGE

AT THE UNIVERSITY PRESS

1950

CAMBRIDGE
UNIVERSITY PRESS

University Printing House, Cambridge CB2 8BS, United Kingdom

Cambridge University Press is part of the University of Cambridge.

It furthers the University's mission by disseminating knowledge in the pursuit of education, learning and research at the highest international levels of excellence.

www.cambridge.org
Information on this title: www.cambridge.org/9781107585744

First published 1950
First paperback edition 2015

A catalogue record for this publication is available from the British Library

ISBN 978-1-107-58574-4 Paperback

CONTENTS

Words are Weak Things	1	Yellow Tulip	25
Just Suppose	2	Dewdrops	26
A Soul to Birth	3	Rather like Rats	26
Secret Passage	4	They	27
Beauty Grows	4	Love and Hate	28
Grief	5	The Lord Walks	31
February 1948	5	Jackdaws	31
Homes	6	The Old Man	32
The Out-of-Balance	7	Man is made a Marvel	33
Formations, Formulations	8	Life and Death	34
Fair Creature	9	Goodness in You	35
Let it Suffice	10	These Days too Few	36
Next Year	11	Part of the Heart of Me	37
I Cannot See	11	Who see the World with Open Eyes	38
Youth and Age	12	
No Miracle's More Mighty	13	Aconite and Snowdrop	39
Golden Moments	14	While the World Darkens	40
Tablets.... A Rebel	16	Bondage	42
On the train to Aberdeen—31st March, 1948	17	Kings Parade	44
		Apologia	45
Withdrawal and Return	18	Birth Immeasurable	46
Emigration	19	The Law	48
A Wonder Men Call Art	20	The Eternal	49
Trinity Fountain. 13th April, 1948	21	Earth and Air	49
		Politics	50
Agreement	22	The Poetic Reaction	52
Those Men	24	Of Our Own Seeing	54

Sick Souls	55	Still Kings and Quiet Queens	76
In a Café	56	Cedar	77
Queer	57	An End	77
Death	57	Cry, 'I'	78
Foreseeingly	58	Neutrality	78
I came to go	60	Belong	79
If	62	Men and Machines	79
Afloat	64	Swallows Returning	80
Almond in Peterhouse	65	How	80
Nothing's to spare	66	Borrowers and Lenders	81
Boykin	67	Starling Song	82
Till Sun Stands at the Zenith	68	Nightfall	83
Stand Out, Stand In	69	Portrait	86
So You Want This	70	Day's End	87
What For?	72	Companions	88
When All are Kings	73	Then shall the Jack Ass Bray	89
If Time be Lent	74	The Preachers	90
Equals	75	Tom Fool's Bottom	91
Moot	75		

To

MARY NEST
and
DAVID

WORDS ARE WEAK THINGS

For the people words are weak things.
Brother, would that we could
Comprehend the ultimate depth
Of minds so many and so unconfined,
So hidden;
Living and growing over the years,
Amassing
So many million loves and fears.
   For the people words are weak things.
Their faces, as of the seaways
Roughened by emotion in endless passage,
Are but the surface of an ocean
Where currents move, and tides.
   For the people words are weak things.
Ten thousand million times
Ten thousand million
Brain cells—the vehicle
Of that unnamed, unnameable—
Not in themselves,
But through the miracle
Of their communion far and near.
   For the people words are weak things.
Brother, shall it be said
That we in isolation
Heart from heart
Can ever have a part,
In Earth's salvation?

JUST SUPPOSE

Just suppose
That you are altogether wrong,
That what you reason out from cause effect
In looking backwards, law,
Is not the only train that runs on rails.

Just suppose
That something more than reason governs ends,
Something more terrible
For good or evil.

These are those forms
'That meet us in the mist,
Coming from lands ahead,
And touch us,
Whispering
'Action'.

A SOUL TO BIRTH

This body full of eyes,
This million-mouthed automaton, myself,
Burning with appetites, prehensile and alight
To eat and solve, down to its elements,
The very clay—yet some time shall see whole!
'It might be', 'It should be', yea 'It must be', do conspire
To regiment and force the wilful lusts and turn
Synoptic gaze on one unfolding view.

    And what are these compulsions that pursue
And integrate the multitude of wills
To give them worth—
But those three Graces of our Lord the King?
Whom, haply meeting, I myself shall fling
Into Hell's fire, this million-mouthed automaton
Thereby to bring
In pain a soul to birth.

SECRET PASSAGE

I do not want to die, do you?
But die you will, and so shall I;
And maybe stand to gain thereby.
Yet once you did, or nearly did,
When nothing worth there seemed to live for.
And then you knew you could not rid
Yourself of self by that escape door;
Yes then you knew
That self and God are one, not two,
And love the secret passage through.

BEAUTY GROWS

Beauty grows! It's not a thing
Man can by his endeavour bring.
His mind must wait on sun and shower
To bring to birth the immortal hour
When from dark death unfolds the flower
That makes the angels sing.

GRIEF

Let there be torn away
This dark deceptive curtain of despair.
The heavy air encumbers, and in grief
Our energies decay.
    Then shall appear
Realities more clear on hillsides far away,
While round us near
Dear lost familiar things
Resume their shape,
From which for long no man did e'er escape.

FEBRUARY 1948

The purple light of evening
Through the bare black bones of trees;
Wind in the heaven blowing
A gale far away on the seas;
Dusk, and the breathing of cattle;
Warm, the damp air of the West;
Earth, the great living mother
Holding us close to her breast.

HOMES

In homes not made with hands we live,
Which seldom solid comfort give.
They will not keep the weather out;
The draughts run through them, in and out,
The wicked squeak, the good man shivers,
The monkey man for ever gibbers.
God give his grace to us poor livers
    In such cold homes to live.

THE OUT-OF-BALANCE

The well-balanced, in perfect health,
Flow smoothly, feeling no problem,
Are, to all intents and purpose, dead.

Time is the out-of-balance,
Generating the opening forces,
The expanding flower.

So we pass out of death into life
To know no ceasing.

Oh, poor soul, seeking rest,
To feel and to think is your burden—

As a boat upon a boundless water
Rides the out-of-balance on a deep of peace—
The Peace of God which passeth understanding.

FORMATIONS, FORMULATIONS

Formations, Formulations,
By Force of Matter
Have no validity
For mind and spirit.

The generative power of these
Is of their very nature,
Sine qua non, and cannot be contained.

So it is curious
That Mind—yea Spirit also—
By force of Matter
Would compel conclusions
And achieve
An End.

FAIR CREATURE

Fair creature, I would see your face
Ever changing, ever new;
Flowering field of God's sweet grace,
In a mortal moment you,
In a mortal moment mine.
Petals light of hair and cheek,
Beauty knowing no eclipse,
Ever there for all who seek,
Star-bright eyes and laughing lips,
Flash of look and turn of feature
Cut for ever out of Time,
In a mortal moment you,
In a mortal moment mine.

LET IT SUFFICE

In a morning of March
Here am I,
In this warm town of old association
And young endeavour of mind and body,
Cambridge.
It might be you.

What want we
(And that other man, also,
Elsewhere)
Growing and flowering in our glory and wholeness
With monstrous imaginings?
Universalism? Totalitarianism?

Do we seek to live on stars, we who live on the earth?
Or do we seek to inhabit molecules?

Are we not little,
So little that nothing can measure our littleness,
Yet so great that we encompass eternity?

Let it suffice,
That I am here
In this warm town of old association and adventure,
Cambridge,
This morning of March that ever is.

NEXT YEAR

Next year, I will have crocuses
    Just there and there,
And daffodils just here amid the grass,
    Next year.

Sunshine in March, bright days of blue,
    And still dry death of yesteryear
    Peeps through;
Reluctant flows the sap before its time is due.

I CANNOT SEE

She said to me:
I cannot see
That there would any difference be
Without the leaven in the bread.
Try it I said.

She said to me:
I cannot see
That all this Christianity
Has made the world the least bit better
Since Jesus died.
Well that, I said, cannot be tried.

YOUTH AND AGE

If young men may be agéd,
Why may not, without offence, the old be skittish?
Twenty, he walks there, look you, heavy of brow,
Awkward on legs unwieldy,
Seeking a stance to swell
With matter of importance.
Quite, yes, quite immortal;
Yet passing short of ready
To meet his drafts on the old skinflint Time.
With care, not all for others,
Doctors and crutches,
He may puff himself but short of bursting.
Prick then that bubble of a sacred self
And down it comes in whistling deflation,
And all his life lies in a wrinkled shroud.

And there is sixty, shrunken,
Light of bone, gay in the infinity of his nothingness.
Equal for him—and merry—
A doodle or an epoch;
The fluid years refresh eternally,
And days and hours are now forgotten coinage,
Young in release, and joyous to enjoy.

NO MIRACLE'S MORE MIGHTY

O moon! so coyly hiding
Behind dark pines and shining
White light on pearly blue.
O tree! so stilly standing
Your limbs through time expanding
The lot of what is you.
O man! what sense is sounding
To know those names astounding
None other ever knew.
O God! whose act is sending
From worlds of now unending
To me, one breaking through.

No miracle's more mighty
Than this bright moonlight view!

GOLDEN MOMENTS

(Dedicated to E. V.)

Things of beauty, how come you?
Thrust forth, or drawn forth?

I am humbled before you,
I am pierced and suffer sharp hurt.
My soul, can you create?
Can you be aligned with your Maker who
    worketh?

My eyes are blind, my ears deaf,
My mind dead.
There is no beauty.
Let there be an end.
So we go down into the night.

Dawn returns in the law of being;
Surges again the light of the holy;
Eyes see, ears hear,
The mind perceives and the spirit
Quivers, muted with understanding.
This light penetrates, raising the dead.
Never thereafter shall they be as before.

From stars, from suns, we know a light,
But not this light.

This light lighting the world,
This light of dawn, ever new
In the law of being,
Springing from Nowhence.

Things of Beauty, how come you?
Thrust forth or drawn forth?

TABLETS...A REBEL

Tablets
And grey stones, flat lying,
Beneath the feet
Of how many men who have trodden the years,
Of how many boys, and girls and women?
Silent and, as ever, still,
Here in the house of worship on the hill.

Earth's bounty without dearth,
A harvest home, I greet,
Think you, a nothing's worth—
No meaning and no matter?
Outside, as ever,
The sparrows sharp and shrill
Make echoing chirp
And chatter,
And wild birds sweetly sing.

Sunshine and shadow's gloom
Fill full the edifice of man's endeavour.
These stony mountain walls,
These rooted pillars,
Support a weight of thought too great
For the light air. They subjugate
The scarce-lit flame of life,
The spirit's glory.

Here once again I will
Subdue and scatter
These petrified abstractions
And renew
My childhood's opening story:
That God, a saving friend can be
On my own level, man (like me)
A unit fighting to be free,
A rebel.

ON THE TRAIN TO ABERDEEN—
31ST MARCH, 1948

Oh, what excitement burned within my breast
To watch that mighty pageant in the west
Of yellow, green, and gold,
In heaven's clear accents told,
High up beyond
Us, in the shadowed earth;
And, central, the red glory of the sun
Rising for ever as it ever sets;
Immortal dawn and deathless eve are one.

WITHDRAWAL AND RETURN

I came to the edge of the forest
In which I had been
Alone
Wandering
Through the dark groves,
Or sitting
In pools of sunshine
Amid the ferns.

I saw in the fields, yonder,
Men
Working,
Moving together slowly
With tools and horses,
Loading a wagon.

Their voices
Came to me over the bridge of the air,
I left the forest and joined them.

EMIGRATION

The seething moment spills,
And forth and onward pours the flood of time.
No longer years expand,
While golden memories
Down through quiet water sinking
Build strong foundations for the growth of man.

So come, Adventure, lively fresh and fickle,
Make all our morrows merry with renewal
Of frolic at each parting of the way,
Our yesterdays a mingling of gay laughter
White foam and gleaming spray.

Repose we shall forget.
The seething moment moves,
And forth and onward pours the flood of time.
Speed on, rough tide,
And never know regret!

Yet would I know the meaning of this haste
Of antic toil and tumult?
Interlaced with what design of goodness
Is it graced, or truth or beauty,
To obligate surrender?

A WONDER MEN CALL ART

It is so very clear
To me that you
Are not a soul or spirit, a quintessence.
You are concrete stuff, a presence
Wholly true,
To love or fear,
To know.
If this be so,
Then God to us, if God there be,
Cannot be else
Than concrete too.
Abstraction has no spur
To vital action,
Whereby the whole
Is focused in a part—
A wonder men call Art.

TRINITY FOUNTAIN.
13TH APRIL, 1948

Out of the hurried fosse of living,
The smell of bodies
And the warm turmoil of the blood in transit,
I came; and sat me on cold stones
Where, with water rustling,
The weaver of silence,
And the sun kissing, gently, reflective,
Perhaps spontaneous, springing from the air,
Would come the lost one.

Many, oh, many are the movements
And many the ways of coming and of going
In a sad world where madness marches
Whither? What rhythm is it runs
Through time to which we dance?

Cool stones
Rounded with much long knowing
Of the deceit of fortune's endless blows,
Speak gently, old ones, a lullaby
To soothe this new born child.

How still and steadfast stands
The everlasting beauty, not ourselves,
Of which we are.

AGREEMENT

On what is outer men can have agreement
By measurement and test: and so they build
The battlements of mind with shapes that fit,
Out of the infinite flux, to meaning for us.
Shadow or substance, term them as you will,
Yet still they stand, tough and impregnable
Against attack of fear or nature's forces,
And furnish forth new armies for our war
To win and hold survival.

       Then through greed and lust
We pour our cup of victory on the dust.

On what is inward no agreement have we.
What's sure, what's steadfast? Can footrules measure
   beauty,
Or Truth in pounds and pennyweights be told,
Or Goodness given instants, minutes, years,
In revolutions like the pulse of worlds,
And so build firm our frameworks? Values these
Native to soul, inherent. No reason have they,
No cause. Say rather are they fountains of all causes,
High courts wherein sad logic holds her pleas,
Suppliant for sanction. Then be judgment given
Which each shall count his dearest goal in action.
      What, say you so?—mere qualities

Subjective, unsubstantial?
           Then back again we swing
To definition, weighing and measuring
Our means, so meaningless, to multiply
For what, not knowing.

THOSE MEN

Those men we know so well,
Whose actions and whose thoughts
Live down the ages
In the eyes and minds of men—
What miracle is this, that what was done
A thousand, nay, two thousand years ago,
Should be so fresh
In vision and in truth!

Something triumphant in the soul
Of those who think and do
Will resonate for ever;
And will one day shatter
Those gaps of time
Which, like white walls of glass,
So fragile, stand between
Us and the mighty past.

Then shall the living mix
And be no longer
Silenced and prisoned
In the ice of years.

YELLOW TULIP

Love lay, white limbed,
On regal bed of roses,
So pale she was and dark eyed,
And near to dying
Away like an echo
Of years gone by.
Gone was the heyday
And the night of magic,
Though faintly imaged yet.

The lithe green pillars
Of the golden-chaliced tulip,
Swaying to the earth's love,
May make love live again
Bright limbed in the still light
Of the young year's dawn.

DEWDROPS

The tiny dewdrops
  In the sun
Make points of light
  To ponder on;
Out of the air they come,
  To go
Back to the air
  In an hour or so.

RATHER LIKE RATS

Train's waiting;
People pushing, walking, and talking
And rushing;
Not very good-looking, most of them,
I must say,
Rather like rats;
Sharply tuned to the moment,
Whiskers twitching,
Short range chaps!

THEY

They are in ambush secretly scheming—
   Men in government offices.
They are in ambush secretly plotting—
   Workers at the benches.
They are in ambush secretly planning—
   Men in the city, men in the boardrooms,
In high places and in low places,
   In foreign capitals.
In the councils, in the churches, and in the hidden
     cells
They are contriving the ruin of me and of mine;
They go about to enslave us and bring us to
     destruction.
Without form or shape, they have no face,
They are altogether evil.
Let us see them and know them!
They.
Who are they not?

LOVE AND HATE

I

This is a shoddy world of lies and dummies
Surcharged with death's infection. See this fellow
Waving his arms, with hair awry, shouts for the moon
All golden in the sky, and straight would have it.
Oh! bon-aventure, let the ranks be formed.
'Tis hate that does it! Shall the moon,
In beauty and cold pride,
Ride thus alone, contemptuous,
And know not hunger, sweat, or the red prick of envy?
Cast her down!
Come robots, come! Out slogans and prevail,
In multitudinous repetition.
For what are lies but truth, or truth but lies?
Grab first and get it. Then shall all be well,
And all in brotherhood and love shall dwell.

II

Yet sure it is, if men pursue new forms
They must encounter the champions of the old.
Then good makes bad, and bad engenders good,
Each girt with self-deception—
And thus the more with passion
The struggle of closed minds is joined.
A robot world of lies surcharged with death's infection.

III

Oh, what is love? A longing for perfection,
Or an intense perception
Of function in the working of a world,
The 'I' with all identified?
But love is will and needs must come to action
So contra must it be as well as pro.
For what is action under power of will
But issue from the choice of Yes or No,
Two ways for ever open side by side.

IV

I saw a lover and his lady,
His heart and soul within him ached,
He suffered always pain for her sake,
Nor would nor could another fate.

I saw a man content and toiling
For home and children with his mate;
His mind was full of facts and planning;
In it there was no room for hate.

I saw his lady always brooding,
Immersed in early tasks and late,
Loving and watching—she, the steersman,
Sensing the compass of their fate.

I saw a boy in far fields working,
Fields fair fashioned by hand of man,
His for the holding. Heart turns over
In awe and love of native land.

I saw a man in office glooming,
His the power of man over man;
Cleansed be his will of hating and loving—
Though sure it is, it never can.

V

Praise be to God for stately mood and phases
   Of evening quietude;
When Love and Hate sink with the sun,
   Their work nigh done,
   In red and golden splendour
Passing far over into the infinite azure
   Of the prelude
And the still majesty of the waiting stars.

THE LORD WALKS

The Lord walks in the High Street;
He sometimes walks with me,
And when he does, my smile is wide
And men are good to see.

The Lord walks in the country,
And when he walks by me
Then is the beauty of the earth
Raised to the nth degree.

The Lord sits in the study,
And when he talks to me
I know the working of the world
And what it's meant to be.

JACKDAWS

The Daws in chuckling eddies
    Come sliding down the sky;
Tell me it's Now that matters
    The Now that does not die.
But men don't seem to wot it,
    And may be that is why
They worry over what is not,
    And tumble down the sky.

THE OLD MAN

There in the hedgerow,
Knees up, hat tilted, all relaxed and still
In sleep,
His hands upon his middle
The old man lay, half sat,
That windless day of sunshine in September
As evening fell.

    Notch under nose, grey hairs on hollow cheek
From point to elbow of the jawbone—
He might have sat there since the birth of time,
An image and a reckoning sublime,
A form, a face, a shell;—

    Which ranging on the seashore
Sets the boy at gaze
In love's amazement,
Sensing life's kinship in the ancient spell
Of beauty's form,
Rare and remote and strange.

    A form, a face, a shell—
Not what it is, what it seems to be,
Has shapen Destiny.

MAN IS MADE A MARVEL

Yes, Man is made a marvel,
Albeit from what's to hand,
And fitted to a framework
That happens there to stand.

The flying oddments settle
To build the pattern true
On a pack of cards that's shuffled
For every man anew.

Yet, by a ray reflected
From regions unsuspected,
Some pieces are rejected
For other shapes selected,
Which fit the pattern too.

The mortal spot-light of the Here and Now
Moves with intention,
Moves in a strange dimension
Of quality and grace.

Thus is he made by chance
And not by chance—
The self's extension
Outside the comprehension
Of Time and Space.

LIFE AND DEATH

Boy, Life is for living!
It will come again,
Each moment bright with joy
Or keen with pain,
Or satisfied with certainty and rest,
All will remain.
    Then let not death—
In fear, or sloth, or crime—
Creep in the framework of a single hour,
Spreading its stinking slime.

GOODNESS IN YOU

So
Your function is
To feel, to know;
And these things are dimensionless,
Yet do possess
Always a quality
Of goodness
More or less—
Goodness in you.
They grow
In truth and beauty
Ever more inward, different, myriadfold,
And rich, in deep degrees of colour—
Call it so—
In range of rhythms passionless and pure
As fire, as snow.
So is the earth's desire
In you
To feel and know;
And for what else is power
But to achieve this hour?

3·2

THESE DAYS TOO FEW

I made these lines for you
 And for myself
To tell us tales of wonder far aloof
From march of days and plod of crushing hoof
 That tramps
 And tramps
Onward forever down the slow decline:
Tales of a land where age is not,
But always change is changeless
And remains
Bright with that knowledge absolute
Of Love's strange light,
Whole and unanalysed,
Nor prisoned jot by jot,
As in these days too few
Daily we die to do.

Rust red of beech leaves,
  Blue green of pine,
Gentle the lap of earth,
  Conscious each line,
Motion made motionless,
  Time without time.
More than reality,
More than a mote of dust,
More than the thought in us,
Part of the heart of me,
Part of eternity
Given thus, taken thus....

Rust red of beech leaves,
  Blue green of pine,
Curve of the earth's lap,
  Conscious each line.

Some men are gifted to arise
And see the world with open eyes.
For most of us,
I grieve to say,
The light of day
Is much too bright; it hurts us.
And would hurt us more
Had we the courage to explore
The Lord's Highway
At high noon-tide,
And face the loss of all our pride,
And know how powerless is our power.
Yet everlasting praise we give,
From some profound instinctive yearning,
For grace of men who do arise
To see the world with open eyes.

ACONITE AND SNOWDROP

The Aconite
Amid dry leaves
Shows once again
Its golden head,
Bright sign of hope born early,
Hardy to shine despite.
    And, round about,
White snowdrops stand serene
In simple glory.
    These two are godlike in the woods;
    They yet are bold,
Though in the misty air
The red sun hovers low,
And all the earth is bare
And cold.

WHILE THE WORLD DARKENS

'While the world darkens
 Listen to the small noises,
  To the small quiet voice;
For I speak to you. I am here.

In the great halls, in the palaces, in the little houses,
The lights which have lighted you,
 Or seem to have lighted you,
 Are going, are dying.
Soon, oh brother, oh sister, comes quickly,
 Comes soon, darkness—
 The darkness utter.
Utterly gone every known and dear companion
 Of wayfaring,
And the doors of your going out and of your coming in
 Will be closed.
The ache of the void will turn to stone
 Your pain beyond pain everlasting—
 It will seem to.
While the world darkens
 Listen to the small voices,
  To the silence;
For I speak to you. I am here.'

'I have no other home,
 But only thee.

As worm the earth I feel my home,
   Dumb, humble, blind
   In darkness of the womb.'

'I am the unmade, I am the made
   I am the Maker.
Behold, I make all things new.
Write, for these words are true.'

BONDAGE

If you will look for Life,
   Then look for Strength;
If Strength, then Structure and Cohesion;
If Structure, Limits, Parts;
   And, if Cohesion,
   Bonds.

Such are the Laws of the Dimensions
Wherein the prowling Self seeks way to find
   Deeper and wider Being,
   And Life from chaos grows:
I speak of Mind and Spirit as of Matter.

Bonds are those energies
   That countervail and stay
   The wayward atom,
And great configurations of joint enterprise
Weave from the limitations
Of a random motion;
The generating stations of their power
Lie deep.
Minds are not free:
Could any man have felt or thought or done
Aught otherwise than as in fact he did?

Maybe a little.

Knowing my bondage, then let me be still
For God to grow, alert to know
The ambivalent will—
For me what will be
Through me, by me, in me.

And would our bondage then be less,
And Beauty fade in formless fusions,
If more in contemplation, less
In action than of old,
Deeper our conscience came to the still deeps
Where love and knowledge interfold?
The answer—Yes? The answer—No?
Both meaningless,
Where no resistance is or stress
In a new conscious whole.

We then agree:
For mind and spirit
Bonds have validity,
Not absolute,
But for us true
In what we feel and think and do;
Each bond of law or logic,
Code or custom,
Or affection,
Gives but a new degree
Of freedom for an entity
In transit t'wards an unconceived perfection.

KINGS PARADE

A wave,
A bus rolls by,
The rush and hush of air
Throb-laden,
Stately on wheels,
A box for bodies
And for souls.

Beyond, above, apart,
Sunlit grey stones
Point to the sky
Where all the quiet of blue abides.
How cold the pinnacles
Man-made and high!
How warm and red the heart!
Servant of God
Pulsing the seconds by
Two thousand million beats
In sixty years,
Who questions how or why!

APOLOGIA

For God
And for all
Whom I love too little
Myself I would whittle away
To the last iota and tittle
In giving and giving—
I would,
If I could,
But I do not.
Forgive
If you can
What I am.

BIRTH IMMEASURABLE

As I walked
I encountered thoughts
Projected,
Reduced to words—
Tokens of meanings,
And the meanings were
In a way
Meaningful to me:
Calm, orderly, and void—
A pattern of white lace.

As I walked
Out of the blue a blow struck me,
Setting the sky aflame
And my head singing.
A blow not from without,
An explosion within,
Self consuming, expanding, spontaneous
    generation of knowledge felt,
A unifying event,
A thought. Whose thought?
Certainly not mine.

A world. Whose world?
Certainly not mine,
Certainly not yours,

Nothing whatsoever at all in it is yours or is mine.
And the answer beyond the thought
Was beyond words
But not beyond knowing,
Not beyond the physiological
Psychic and spiritual comprehension
Of the body.

THE LAW

What is the Law?
Law is to give, give all.
Freely, no man can give:
Only the Highest Good
Gives without taking.
By false accountancy
Man may himself deceive,
But not that One
Upon the judgment seat;
So lawless things go back
To formless seas of promiscuity.
Let it be known,
Conceit full blown
May seem
Much to achieve, in violence of decay,
Through strife.
What is the Law?
The Law is living Will
Alway that loveth
And worketh where it may,
Than which no other way
Leadeth through death
To Life.

THE ETERNAL

In the market place was the Eternal,
      in the mid morning;
A face, huge, bland, transparent
      to all that can ever be,
A face from which the Inscrutable peered
      with eyes that see;
And every feeling that can ever be felt,
      or knowledge sensed,
Was in that single countenance.

EARTH AND AIR

In the detachment of my presence
I have always been moving
Amid the moving grass and the long daisies;
Moving with the ripple of the air
The ripple of the soft bending grasses
At the interface
Of earth and of air,
Systems immiscible
Yet particulate
To interpenetrate, where
Each is in orientation of conscious order,
And random nature is checked.

The definition of order,
And the winning of men's hearts
To willing subordination
And joyous abandon
   In the figured dance,
In which they move functionally
In the determined and lawful
Harmonies of interweaving pattern,
Neither exploiting nor exploited,
And without feeling or cause to enquire
Into purpose, as reason demands
From mistaken confusion
Of means with ultimates,—
   This is the Divine
Working in our conscious being,
And is to be reverenced.
   The joy of the dance
Is in giving and in the perfection of action,
In surrender to the mystery of Nonself
Greater than Self,
And so to escape from the little locked cell
Into the wide arena,
Into the wider, into the all-embracing
   rhythms,
With the casting away of inhibitions,

Which indeed are but the baby clothes
Of earlier beginners.
  And Everyman in his dance
Performeth the measures of many interweaving orders,
Yet the political order is, as it were,
The moving and fluid skeleton supporting all,
In which Each always has had his part.

THE POETIC REACTION

What is the poetic reaction
To the days that unfold,
To the days of our life,
To the on-running and flowing away
Of this inconceivable wavering ocean of experience,
This firmament of our sensations particulate,
Leaping out suddenly, myriad bright, unexpected,
   never the same in repetition,—
And fading into the mist?

The ocean of the on-coming and of the passing
   away
Shall be divided and measured
In delayed responses;
And the fragments shall show an appearance of
   order
Of kinds and of classes,
Feelingly distinguished,
Knowledgeably partaking of the quality
Of that which is to be sought,
Of that which is to be avoided;
Yet not in abstractions
Of words or of symbols or of facts which
   vanish
Is the poetic reaction.

The poetic reaction
Is the formation of forms in response
Not to be communicated nor had at second-hand,
Nor measurable, but eternal and certain,
The penetrating activity of absolute acceptance,
The home-coming of rest in the unity of love and of
    knowledge,
The in-being of the holy.

And the quality of our poetic reaction
Is the quality of our life.

So what shall be felt
And known and seen
In the poetic reaction
Shall also appear and be done;
As the heart of oak grows,
As the hurdler soars, sliding like a wave,
As the dog lies in the sun, and the mountains dream,
As the builder builds the house of the Lord
Nor reckons the years in his patience,
As the eager mind draws near, and falls back,
And again draws nearer,
As the rain and the wind purify,
As anger mounts the black tower and flashes blindingly,
As the lie perishes in its own pit,
As the sea smiles and laughs to heaven in comradeship,

As the music makers speak with tongues,
As age harvests wisdom in peace,
And the beauty of youth multiplies loveliness,
As the glories of the morning and of the noon day
Consummate union at the going down of the sun,
As comes at last the luminous darkness of night
Gathering into its one self
The manifold images of day.

OF OUR OWN SEEING

If aught there be distinct,
Then it can have no action.
It must be
Unknown, unknowable:
And all that's known,
Has been, or will be,
Suffers in knowing change.
We walk a world of our own seeing
Which never's twice the same.
Its quality is inward;
Inward its every name.

SICK SOULS

Sick souls, sick souls,
I bid you silence keep.
You stink in your decay;
Your putrid breath
Erupts in speech,
Bitters the common way
Of common folk,
Who fear not death,
Who know the joy of strife,
Clean gotten into life
And quick.
Silence I bid you keep;
Or they will lay
The knife to your pale shoots,
And take them to the burning heap.

IN A CAFE

At two he came;
I did not know his name.
His long thin nose
And magical lidded eye,
Merry and clever,
So *sotto voce*,
Mirthfully questioning why
Was I, were you.
A gentle joke,
The bloom upon the grape,
A million reasons why—
But none that matter!

QUEER

Illogical—
Not to say queer—it is
To contemplate catching
And comfortably confining
The Lord God Almighty
In a logical net
Of your own designing.

DEATH

Death, calm and cold,
Upon a slab of stone.

Something not seen before is here,
A strangeness utterly unknown,
The stranger that its shape is shown
So like, yet so unlike, its own
When life was there.

Dear known one
Thou art gone,
And I stand here
Alone.

FORESEEINGLY

Foreseeingly
The man puts by for future need,
The tree puts forth its greenery,
The peoples build conformities.
Our physics and our chemistry
Know not responses such as these.

The germ
Its microstate of molecules adapts,
By means unlearned, unknown,
Not just to this or that
Of passing impact,
But to processional encounters
Twixt its inherent theme
To multiply and stretch to strange extreme
Its unit forms
Serving one body,
And the on-coming hazards yet to be
Of this revolving world about the sun.

Then come
These conscious minds,
Locked singly in brains of single men,
Building the pattern of events
From moving idols seen

In that strange hall
Where living cells do think.
No longer then the germ
Slow-moving over centuries,
But the quick mind in moments
Operates, responds
To what will be,
Is purposive.

In its own likeness
Germ begets germ;
Likewise after its kind
Mind begets mind.

And is there not,
Borne on the waves of ether or of air,
A confluence of thought with thought,
In constellations linking brain with brain,
Each to its strange extreme extending,
Serving One Mind,
And some still stronger foresight
In this last incarnation?

I CAME TO GO

I always thought—
And now I know—
My life is short;
I came to go.
What terror then
Can endless time
Bring more to men,
Whose little mind
Can comprehend
One nought no less
No more than nine?

Shall the day's peep,
When birds asleep
Twitter a faint
Sad far off cheep—
Shall the day's dawn,
When song is born
And sun leaps up
And night is gone—
Shall summer's noon,
Which steals too soon
In silence over
Hill and coombe—
Shall eventide,

Which opens wide
The heart to all
The grace of God—
Shall these abide?

I shall not know
Till comes that day
When I must go.

IF

If,
Left to themselves,
Chemical reactions
Have built these eyes,
These seeing eyes,
Those fine enamelled teeth,
That golden hair—
Flower of breath-taking fragrance—
Those round and unripe breasts,
Those feeling finger tips, those lips, those thighs
To function mated,
Then say I, they have know-how!
They have more sense
Than scientists allow.
Somewhere there slips
Out through the weave of formulae
The quick,
Faster than light.
Nothing may prison it.
So, in the body's building,
Must be wit—
Steering committees
And selection boards,
Selecting the highly improbable;
Perversity, too,
And unethical behaviour

Among atoms
As such.
More's in this bit of body
Than's declared
In the whole height of heaven
Crowded with dusty light
Of aeons spent.

AFLOAT

Catspaws on surface
Of a glassy deep
Creep, crisp and fade.

The strong long undulations
Onward sweep.
Unseen they come
In swoon of sleep;
Yet on and on their way they keep.

    The storm
    That bade them rise
    Tore its fierce life
    From patient skies.
    As anger dies
    It died.

But these live on,
To cradle keels
Of lives upon
The ocean wide,
And crash in splendour
On the earth's last steep.

ALMOND IN PETERHOUSE

The naked knife of Beauty
Biteth deep.
Beauty of Earth—Beauty of Earth!
Beyond tears,
Beyond heartache!
Intake of breath
Shatters the self's full ease
To pertinent nullity:
Oh, lovely One,
In your absolute Otherness!

NOTHING'S TO SPARE

Have a care! Have a care!
Bodies touch bottom,
Souls have no ceiling
Up there.
What is needed
For procreation
Is little:
What is needed
For love
Is not little—
Much too much
For enough
Is needed,
And
Nothing's to spare.

BOYKIN

Where are your roots,
   Boykin?
I have no roots, Father;
I'm new as a new pin.
All byegones are byegones to me, Father.
   When I begin,
   I begin.

TILL SUN STANDS AT THE ZENITH

More bees, more workers;
So the hives in spring
Make bees as men make men,
Saving no surplus of their food supplies,
All is put back again:
All gain, hard won, is lost
To raise more fetchers-in.

So the days lengthen as the hive extends,
Till sun stands at the zenith.

Then down hot days of drowse
And honey hum
Through June, and by July,
And on to August
Creeps a change.
The workers spare their care
To build ever more bees and more:
They now pile surplus higher,
And still higher.

So are bees wise,
For always summer dies,
Always does winter come.

STAND OUT, STAND IN

You can stand out;
You can stand in.
Stand out,
With analytic eye
And view well calculated,
And you may see,
Or seem to see in dream,
The tiniest part,
And how related,
Of all so far remitted in the scheme
Of things created.
Stand in,
With synergetic vim,
And you may bring
New wholes to being,
You may win
To things undreamed of:
But will be,
Beyond redeem,
Committed
By them, to them, in them.
I will not dare to say—
Will you?—
Who gains more praise
At end of day,
In God's purview.

SO YOU WANT THIS

So you want this,
And you want that.
You can, in fact,
Do one thing or another;
And then will have
One thing, not t'other.

A simple thing to say
Today, as on any day
Since Eve was first a mother.

And when it's done, it's done.
Then faith maintains
That law remains
Inviolate.

'Tis done, so clearly could be,
Nor could have been
Aught otherwise;
Cause and effect
Related;
And so would be again
(Though this cannot be checked)
If ever once again
In that same way

Should that same cause
Obtain—
Which is not likely.

Well, howsoever
That may be,
This we'll agree—
   Something weighs down the scales,
   Something decides
   Which Want prevails,
   Which Life survives.

WHAT FOR?

The impetuous urge to do
Surges and pounds
Within the heart.
No rest. No rest.
Time is not blessed;
'Tis cursed.
To make, to make, where nothing was before,
Cities to populate,
Wheels to set turning,
And all the flood of nature to shore up
And keep contained;
Building with all that's done
A workhouse for more doing.
Stop! Think!
Little man! Little woman!
These millions and these millions more—
Must it go on for ever—
Can it go on for ever?
And what for?

WHEN ALL ARE KINGS

When kings were few
The damage they could do
Was not too great
For nature to allay and renovate.
When all are kings,
And all desires
Must be filled up,
What then?
Now is the spate
And overspill of aeons
Pulsing and pouring to acquire
Beauty and power.
In one short hour
What aeons built
Is spent.

IF TIME BE LENT

If time be lent,
Let us do less,
Live more
In joy of simple life;
Be blest in sacrament,
Not cursed in everlasting strife
And war.
O Book of wonder!
Which our Self perceives
Through Its bright instruments
When these
Not on ourselves are focused.

EQUALS

As I trod the warm earth
When the light was fading
In the garden of trees
Where the buds were waking
Silent and still against the sky,
I thought of equations
Of man's mad making
To help him to rule
And to help him to die;
For nothing is equal that lives,
And the glory of living is shed
From the great on the less,
From the low on the high.

MOOT

Innately
Bodies and minds
In congress and in conference
Seek loot,
How each most may receive,
Least give....
In joining their variety of powers,
Least action is the law of moot.

STILL KINGS AND QUIET QUEENS

They stand
The tulips red
And the yellow wallflowers,
Still kings and quiet queens:
And by them passes
The beating of dead feet
Upon the pathways.

The tearing rape of rubber on the tarmac
Shrieks. Is gone.
An instant moment
Leaps from the lap of God.

Compass us quickly,
Sparkle of divine insight;
Crown us with fire,
As have been these
That were unseen,
Bright kings and golden queens.

CEDAR

Cathedral of shadows,
Liquid, limpid Cedar,
Fluid in the rain-washed
Sweet-smelling air!
I pass; you stay
And stand here,
Winter and summer, night and day,
New sign to each newcomer
Who comes here,
Halts here,
And then goes on his way.

AN END

And if there is an end
I do not want an end—
I do not want it!

CRY, 'I'

To sacrifice
By mere neglect
Is not self giving;
For love is will,
That living we may give and get
More, and more yet,
To life—from life.
So, climbing to the crest of hill,
In high defiance will I still
Fling challenge to the Devil's skill:
Cry, 'I'. Cry, 'I am I'.

NEUTRALITY

They nod,
Wagging their heads:
Knowledge, they say,
Is neutral;
And scholars take an oath
Against all wishful thinking.
    Let knowers know
That this same wishful thinking
Stands as the one thing known.
Then will they be more men and more
Like God.

BELONG

We belong to you, and you to us,
As brother to sister, son to mother,
In mutual ownership of home.
Our soil is home to you, and yours to us.
Your land to us is otherwise than foreign.
So freely o'er the earth we pass,
Servants and masters of our lot and way.

MEN AND MACHINES

When one man
Has many tools,
Then is he king and master.
When one man
Has one tool,
And one machine
One minder,
Then are the two
Well matched.
But one machine
With many minders
Binds men
To servitude.

SWALLOWS RETURNING

Next to no summer
Comes e'er the comer
Comes o'er the sea and
   Skims o'er the down.
Swallow-pairs fleeting,
Frolic in greeting,
Roll on the wing as
   They wing o'er the down.
Swallows returning
Yearn to their homing,
Turn in the wind as
   They turn o'er the down.

HOW

There is a way
Of saying something new
That makes it seem
You always knew it known.

There is a way
Of treating an old theme
That makes it seem
The latest talk from town.

All men are all men's debtors.
Say,
Till debtors pay their debts,
May they
Give gifts?
Oh, sorry sight of all men living;
No one has that—
For honest giving!
And, tell me this,
If all men lend,
May each foreclose
At will,
To spend?

STARLING SONG

The starling on the chimney pot
Was singing to himself a lot.
The rippling chatter of his note
Raised all the feathers on his throat
   Like tiny quills,
His beak and body never still,
His eye round roving low and high,
He seemed on springs about to fly;
His eye round roving high and low,
Apt to an instant call to go;
   But no. But no.
   And still and still
He wheezed and whistled through his bill
   His very active thought.

NIGHTFALL

Always to be
In some other place,
In some other time,
Than in this place
And in this time
(In which all is contained)
Is me.
I would cease,
Yet would I not cease.
I am content to go out into Not-being,
Yet am I not content
To accept
Only the oneness of eternity.

*　　*　　*

This night,
This tree,
This larch in summer's dress,
Single and finite,
Black
Imprint upon the golden glowing west,
Exalts in me
The motionless triumph
Of its delicate sharp darkness,
An infinity of revolution
Compact into stillness.

I see
The twinkle of the flitter-bat,
Down, up,
Round and down.
As I, so my father,
And my father's father,
And his father,
Have seen it against the sky,
This lucid sky of summer's night.

Over in the wood there,
Hark! The owl
('Now! Now!')
Hangs moonlight pearls
Upon the ear of silence,
Lonely and everlasting.

And, when I turn,
The pines, in open order,
Have advanced and stand
Immanent,
Dark and deathless,
In the deep-burning blue of the portal.

*   *   *   *

Always to be
In some other place,
In some other time,
Than in this place

And in this time
(In which all is contained)
Is in me, mortal,
My elliptical duality,
The itch.
Without which,
Perhaps nothing!
I would cease,
Yet would I not cease.
I am content to go out into Not-being,
Yet am I not content
To accept
Only the oneness of eternity.

PORTRAIT

Black silk, white lace,
Dark hair, clear eyes, pale face:
A life is living in that portrait there,
Which draws me into stillness, as I stare
Across the centuries. And now and here
Her person and her presence touch my own,
An unknown woman—but for ever known.

    *   *   *   *

And should the assiduous antic analyse
The airy space between her youth and mine
He might disclose much motion, tell no lies
Yet speak no word of truth.

DAY'S END

The sky hangs high
And grey and still,
Filled with frail moisture;
A mist is damp on the hand;
The stiff pines stand
In rigid posture;
The tender larch sprays, pendent,
Undulate and sway
Gently a little, now and then.

A sudden breath
Sets poplar leaves a-sighing,
As slow seas sigh
On shingle strand.

Silence impending,
I sit and see and listen,
And birds sing sadly;
For the day is waiting,
Waiting—just waiting—
For the day's end.

COMPANIONS

Once at sunset
With my dear one
Hand-in-hand,
Down the lane and
Up the meadow
Through a land
Not of that world,
Nor of this world,
I meandered;
For its magic
Landscape lingered,
Ever lingers,
Lingers,
And
In that dreamland
Ever-present,
Never-ending,
We in sunshine,
We in shadow,
Still meander
Hand-in-hand.

THEN SHALL THE JACK ASS BRAY

Freely
In many realms
Will man with man agree,
Himself be
The lesser in degree
Of skill in work or play
Than many another;
But, if we say,
What then shall be the way
To manage our affairs in common,
Or contemplate our destiny,—
Then shall the owl hoot and the Jack Ass bray
And folly quick with wisdom quarrel.

THE PREACHERS

I saw a woman much bedizened
Curiously preaching righteousness.
'Twas hard to tell what nature made her
So much of artifice o'erlaid her;
But with the young or simply credulous
She went down well, did this old belle.

I saw a man with all his clothes off
Curiously preaching righteousness.
'Twas hard to know what nature thought him,
His antics did so much distort him;
But with the young or simply credulous
He went down well,
Did this old wizened bird of hell.

In harmony I heard one voice:
'Power is the Glory, Power is the Way,
Obey! Obey,
Or be cast out!
Yours is the choice!'

Thus did these preachers blend
Their many different words
To one same end.

TOM FOOL'S BOTTOM

My reputation, I would say,
Among the brethren today,
Never too high, is now as low
As Tom Fool's bottom.
But never mind,
My loves are free;
I find
Them kind;
And in my heart is frolic.

Printed in the United States
By Bookmasters